About the Author

A wonder who is interested in the mystic art of Sufism.

Eros

Mo The Sage

Eros

Olympia Publishers
London

www.olympiapublishers.com
OLYMPIA PAPERBACK EDITION

A CIP catalogue record for this title is
available from the British Library.

ISBN: 978-1-83543-057-6

This is a work of fiction.
Names, characters, places and incidents originate from the writer's
imagination. Any resemblance to actual persons, living or dead, is
purely coincidental.

First Published in 2025

Olympia Publishers
Tallis House
2 Tallis Street
London
EC4Y 0AB

Printed in Great Britain

Dedication

To all those who are deeply in love

Acknowledgements

I'd like to thank Rumi and Attar for inspiring me to write.

Dear Sir/Madam

I am writing to you in regards of an opportunity of us working together to create something beautiful.

After jumping headlong into inspiration, I have created something which is close to my heart, forty poems of love (eros) and separation which are influenced by writers such as Rumi, Ibn Arabi and Hafiz. These poems have a mystic touch to them as they follow the laws of the religion of love. After many readings and Sufi practices, I had a dream that I should follow this path of writing and create inspirational poems for the rest of my life. Therefore, I am hoping to reach many more people with these poems and create a following of the religion of love, so with your help we can start the journey of a hundred thousand step.

I do not have any experience in writing, it was just a dream which got me moving into this direction; however, my father was a writer and a newspaper publisher back in Tanzania, which means writing is in my blood and it is something that brings peace of mind and I would like to do it for the rest of my life. Therefore, if you take a risk and publish my book, I will be a loyal comrade and I will stay with you for the rest of my career, this can lead to an amazing partnership that can break into the new world.

My profession is currently in management and have been in management for the last eleven years; however, I have been really interested in leadership, reading many books to improve my understanding of the phenomenon of great men and women in history with this knowledge that I have gathered. I would like my writing to influence people to be better in themselves and become the bridge to the next generation as Friedrich Nietzsche said. With this knowledge, the poems which are written are meant to cure the gap that is left in the heart when separation from loved ones is caused. So, I hope to touch people's mind deeply and to show them that their suffering is not isolated by a universal cause when you love intensely.

Love is a powerful emotion, that is why, I dived headlong into exploring this in the poems and create a connection with lust which comes into when one first falls for the opposite sex or whatever their preference. So, these poems take a religious touch into them; however, they can be called somewhat sinful as they show the ugly side of love, or more worshipping breaking into idol mode which the religion of love goes against. Knowing this, I wanted to link the understanding that God can be whatever the eyes fall for and is the manifestation of the purest love that we have. So, my poems describe the most desperate form of someone who desires and misses his lover and is willing to do anything it takes to win them back, as the experience of being without them is unbearable. It goes to describe the loved one as God and uniting with them is the only thing the lover wants; this can be interpreted as sexual or spiritual union which we all do after death or when we reach enlightenment. Some poems are about poverty as one is willing to take something as an outcome of gaining the beloved; this is one of the greatest fear in the new world; therefore, it shows that one is willing to suffer greatly just for the beloved to take interest in him or her again.

So, with all that I have said, I hope you will be excited about what will come in the future and now as you publish this book. With time, as the vineyard grows ripped grapes for the finest wine, so will my skills as a poet will grow and greater poems will come out of the unknown and grab the mind of readers; therefore, do not just think that it will be a one-off creation but a lifetime of work that you are investing in.

Bismillahir Rahmanir Raheem

I tremble without you
Lovesick, and I miss you
I have tasted you a hundred, thousand times
And every time I want you more
I am just a poor street beggar
You! A monarch to my love
Every day, I come asking for a glance
Or some more
After it is done, I am empty
Hoping you will always provide me with more
Do not ration your daily touch
Without it, I will fade into nought
The saints say that is what I need
But who asked for their advice?

Bismillahir Rahmanir Raheem

You are as sweet as sugar
I seek you after every meal
I can never get enough of you
You're in my coffee early in the morning
You're in my tea late at night
Sweat overcome me when I am without you
Reduced to an infant without milk
Loud lamentation they hear from me
What's life without her
To escape into paradise
Is to be with you as bees are with honey.

Bismillahir Rahmanir Raheem

One glance is not enough, I need more
One verse is not enough, I need more
One touch is not enough, I need more
Just as a fish needs water, I need you
So, a hundred thousand times a day, I look into your radiant
eyes
So, a hundred thousand times a day, I write words to describe
your rosy cheeks
So, a hundred thousand times a day, our lips are in union
When will I be satisfied, only God knows.

Bismillahir Rahmanir Raheem

Let us meet in the rose garden,
Where the clouds are nowhere to be seen
And the sun is shining oh so brightly
Where the ear is intoxicated by the songs of the nightingales
Which songs can they be but those of union with the rose?
Being with the rose is the tulip's desire
The rose holds the centre stage at every garden
Its beauty is that of the beloved
So, being with the rose is my only desire
You're the rose in my heart's garden
Blooming in remembrance of you
Five times a day or more
I am having to keep you in my prayers
So that I may be with you in this world and that to come.

Bismillahir Rahmanir Raheem

Oh, Mrs Shiva
You make my heart go *boom, boom, boom*
Like every machine that can kill
You make my heart go *boom, boom, boom*
Like a machine can ever kill me
Oh, Mrs Shiva
Without you, there isn't a reason for my existence
Only in remembrance of you am I living
Five times daily, I am in prostration
In the hope that our flesh can be united
Oh, Mrs Shiva
Why don't you just leave him
And join me in this religion of love
Where the cupbearer brings tall glasses full of lust
And our passion can burn brighter than the sun
Oh, Mrs Shiva
A hundred thousand times can never be enough
As long as I am breathing
Ill sip the wine and get intoxicated by your essence
Know that I am Majnun and you're my Layla.

Bismillahir Rahmanir Raheem

I have seen Mother Nature
She is, oh, so beautiful!
She is just like how you are
Face as charming as the new moon
Pleasant blue or maybe hazel eyes
Cheeks radiating the hue of roses
Lips sweeter than milk and honey
Frame so slender, just like a cypress tree
Oh, my moon-face one
How your beauty has pierced my heart
Everywhere I look, there is only you to be seen
So, I prostrate myself to you
Is that blaspheme, you say
In bewilderment, I have torn my coats many a times
Searching the answer to it all
If I am an idolater, then I am not afraid to be
I am not bent on statues or a multitude of you
I feen for every single atom of your existence
Maybe if Iblis was asked to prostrate himself before Eve
He would have done it, just as I am doing
Al-Basir, can you not see
She is more than human
She is more than an angel
She is more of a creator
Moulding me to be the superman as Nietzsche expanded

At night, I become a beast
And I am overwhelmed by lust
She does things that quench my thirst
Like pouring the wine into my cup
So I drink, so I drink, so I drink
Greed causes the highest level of intoxication
And when we start to dance
She lets me pull back on her tress
Her moans sound like nightingales in the dawn of spring
Causing ecstasy to flood the bed we are in
During the day
She beams brighter than the sun's ray
Exposing all the shadows to be a void
Illuminating clearly the path
And all my want for pleasure dies to the way
By her commend, I go beg for my daily bread
So I can stay living and utter these verses of her glory
According to the beloved, you can have her too
But my jealousy is wrath
As she is my Helen and you can't handle a Trojan War.

Bismillahir Rahmanir Raheem

My moon-face one
You are like milk and honey
Your flesh is as soft as halwa
The sweet tooth in me tells me to take a bite
Don't you worry, I will be gentle
Slowly savouring all your charms
Before we start, let us put wudu
And curse Iblis with a bismillah
Let us hide under a veil
I do not want another soul to know
These are the most intimate prostrations
And my greed for you has only increased my appetite
Every single atom of your halwa-like flesh is mine
From one side to the other side of the plate you will be spread
Is it for my or your pleasure?
That my finger moves up and down during Tashahhud
By pulling you closer to my mouth
My tongue will be dancing eloquently at each verse
All my tastebuds you will excite
Gasp... gaps... gasp
The beloved has said that patience is a virtue
So, as a good slave, I only follow those advices
Before jumping headlong into much deeper bites
I will utter words to Ar-Rahim
To soften the pain and increase our pleasure

The question is how much you can endure
You say, till the is nothing left behind
And the plate is wiped clean
The only way to explain our union is this
That you're the fuel to my fire
By following the religion of love
I know by consuming your halwa
It turns into nonexistence in this material world
And is resurrected in my body and it became a part of me.

Bismillahir Rahmanir Raheem

I have been jumping headlong into the deepest sea
In the hope to find a pearl as beautiful as she is
She is the sweetest girl that I have ever seen
Even her skin looks like it's been covered by the cocoa bean
Eyes like those of a gazelle, oh, so mysteriously!
Thighs as thick as tree trunk, oh, so suggestively!
Hair that flows like the river Ganges
But I am just a poor beggar in these streets
How can I obtain a meeting with such a one?
But when I find that pearl, I will be a scholar by the king
So, I prostrate myself to Al-Hakeem
In the hope he brings wisdom, which brings me closer to that
pearl
I think of the many things I will do
Once I am united with my love
Every moment I am separated for her
Is like I am suffering through a hundred thousand hells
I am left with nothing but lust
How my imagination is showing me all these pictures of us?
One moment we are kissing
Another moment we are doing yoga like Adam and Eve
The same moment our sweat causes a hundred rose bushes to
grow
Whilst your wailing tunes that initiate jealousy to the
nightingale
These are all of my deepest desires.

Bismillahir Rahmanir Raheem

I see our future
In her radiant eyes
Her rosy cheeks
Tell me
That she is in delight
These sweet verses
Will soon run out
So, I prostrate myself to the moon
So she can let me pull out this demon tool
Only she knows
I am Iblis!
And the rest are nothing but imitations
This art is oh so clean
Yet, oh so filthy
Do not fear
The sun is no longer here
And the night patrol is nowhere to be found
So, it is just me and you
I brought gasoline
And a match for your passion
I will set the whole of you on fire
Not even the ocean
Can quench that flame
Can you feel it?
This hand peels flesh

This tongue colder than ice
This tool left her forsaken
So, go on, run to the monastery
See if your god can save you.

Bismillahir Rahmanir Raheem

Come, we scatter roses
And beautify the garden to your delight
Beautiful things to a beautiful one
So, I prostrate myself to Al-Wadud
In the hope that we can share that love
Will he accept my verse?
Even so I utter them in a trance
We have been intoxicated by that wine
Causing her to grind and sing a song
And our heads are lost in dancing
We have turned this *dunya* into Jannah
She is my alchemist.

Bismillahir Rahmanir Raheem

Her eyes, like those of a lioness
Piercing a thousand hearts
With a single glance, kings cheer
With one flicker of her eyelashes
A whole world is ransacked
To look at
She is the full moon
Yet, when it comes to stealing my heart
She is Layla
Under the dark shadow of her hair
Her face is a lamp or rather a torch
With ravens weaving their wing around it
Overwhelming sweetness flows through her mouth
Is it possible, then, to break the veil of existence with a grain
of sugar?
She really does not need nude
The milk she drinks turn rose colour at her lips and cheeks
The pen is weak, better stop now.

Bismillahir Rahmanir Raheem

I whisper into the wind
Of the love, I have for you
It is something I cannot explain
Something I can only show you
So, why don't you come a little closer
And meet this sinner half way
I have studied the Sufi
And I am trying to live that way
It's the religion of love, so loving you is the right way
I give up many things to get closer to the way
I give up my house, my career and my wealth
So I can write verses to glorify you
It is so intoxicating, it leaves the elephant dizzied for days
So, what chance do I have but to be lost by the wine cup?
So, in bewilderment, these verses come to me
And I sing them out load to nobody
But I know he is always listening
So, these verses are really prayer
That I keep near to my heart
In the hope that they polish it
So that love can return, and I see you again.

Bismillahir Rahmanir Raheem

Five daily prostrations
Followed by a hundred thousand kisses sent your way
You see, you're the only reason for my being
So, every moment I breathe, gratitude must be given
I have been wiping this mirror over and over again
Wishing that it can reflect the essence of you
I would be lying if I said one moment is all I need
But I want to be mingled with the whole of your existence
Patience is a virtue
Consistence is clarity
So, I have been observing patiently, your like and dislikes
And I have been consistently practicing the verses that might
capture you
But the devil keeps putting obstacles before me
Like can you see, the multitude out there
This one beauty is all in her face
That one beauty is all in her thighs
That one beauty is in her behind
Your love can be spent elsewhere
Where you do not have to worry of how many you give to
But just like he is, I am prideful
If I am to bend the knee, then it must be to you
It is not just for your rosy cheeks
Or for your eyes that are the pearls of the ocean
Or for your lips, for being so sweet like honey

Or for your frame, for being so nimble like a cypress tree
It's the command you have over my nature
You make me better than I am
Just in remembrance of you, I become superman
Our union turns me into the beast
At one moment and an angel at the same moment
I want to be between nonexistence and existence
 So, making love with you makes me reach that moment
Therefore, I do not see duality, there can only be one Layla
And I am suffering the pain of separation for her
Every moment the devil says to quench my lust
But he does not see what I see
The road is hard, the valleys are dangerous, but I meet what is mine
There is too much to talk about here, let's go to another.

Bismillahir Rahmanir Raheem

It is not you that I am loving
It is her
She is in everything that I see
Furthermore, she is in everyone that I meet
Her gentle smile shine through
All the friendly faces that I see
So, I am never far from her
Whenever I want to meet her
I close my eyes and go into the garden
The beautiful rose has her essence
Playing love game with the nightingale
The pain is, I know you're a part of me too
It's just I don't know how to tap into that
How joyful would life be
If I meet the one.

Bismillahir Rahmanir Raheem

Forty days I am fasting
So I can see your essence
Only when I am rendered to nothing
Do you show yourself
Your beauty is unreal
And once I gaze at you
Life surges up in my body
You're always with me
But only show yourself when I am lamenting and in pain
So, I wonder, should I challenge myself more?
I think you want a champion
Who goes through suffering in this world
You have said this world is nothing but a plaything
But the scars are real to me
I would rather be at bliss
Mingled within you
Cuddling and feeling your flesh
But I guess that's not the man you're after
You want a masculine man, who can defeat a lion
Whilst his penis is still erect
So I sit with the Sufi
Working on verses that will intrigue you
And preparing the mind for that lion
All the art is for nature, and you make her jealous.

Bismillahir Rahmanir Raheem

All these prostrations
Are really making the body nimble
All these verses
Are only increasing the thoughts
Once I have you in union
You best be ready for the most wicked
Bismillah and Iblis is cursed
This is heavenly love
Where God said he never burdens a man with more than he
can handle
So, let me tell you
Can you really handle this?
Oh my moon-face one
Let me give you my glow like the sun has
Have you melt like snow does
You've been walking around
With a chip on your shoulder
Like the son of Adam is really not fierce
I am here to show you
That was Iblis' downfall
So, let me be the judge and hand down the punishment
I will send you to hell but the feeling is oh so heavenly
There are seven levels, but all we need is three
I will put you at Al-Hawiya where the lips and tongue take
command

You will feel them from your throat all the way to your thighs
Then in Al-Jahim where the finger eclipses the moon
Moving side to side until water gushes out
It will be like rain that the meadows need
Finally, let's jump to *Jahannam* where the tool is at best use
How much will you suffer till your toes curl up?
One moment gazing into your eyes
The next moment pulling on your tress
Is this what is meant by yoga?
Have you been practicing like the idol-worshiping Hindu?
All these verses are blasphemy
But what is Islam without blasphemy
What is a sinner to Al-Ghafoor?

Bismillahir Rahmanir Raheem

Call the cup bearer
And ask them to pour the wine
I am missing my lover
But the beloved is in us all
So, when I am intoxicated
I am in union with you all
So, let me dance fiercely
And chant profligately
My chest is torn apart
But my lungs are heavy with air
So I can shout these verses
Till they reach the seven heavens
Give me more wine
Till I reach oblivion.

Bismillahir Rahmanir Raheem

Oh sweet one!
Your tress smells so fragrant
Like sweet lilies on a summer's day
I have fallen so deep into worshiping you
That I have exchanged the mosque
For this cosy pub
But I keep my verses with me
Because after all, it is the religion of love
Even Rumi used to get the wine for a Christian friend
There is no difference, we are all united under one roof
So, if I devote myself to your form like a Hindu
Know that Iblis has become my companion
And all I want is to kiss you
And do more than that
But since we are getting intoxicated
And singing songs of love
I can say to Iblis that three is a crowd
It is hard to get rid of him when you're oh so fine
A thought comes to take your hand
Pull you closer and just grind
Bismillah curses Iblis
So the tool doesn't rise up
All these thoughts
Is what really keeps me away from that path
Oh, dear beloved!

How can I make myself pure?
I am suffering from this *dunya*
Her hips keep me bewildered
But if I read lbn Arabi I am lost in the same sense
I want to be a Sufi but she is so delightful
And I am in a culture where the wine is so sweet
And these love songs are so profligate
So watch my verses, they might be blasphemes
But they always lead me to the right path.

Bismillahir Rahmanir Raheem

All these verses
Fall below your lovely face
How do I describe you without describing paradise?
Being in you is the feeling that we are all after
If a get a feel of it, then I am in Jannah
Therefore, I throw prostration to make sure I enter it
In remembrance of the one, your face comes into my mind
You're the spirit of the spirits, not the spirit of the pot
Pure nectar like *Sharaban Tahuran*
One sip of you and I enter bewilderment
I am just a madman
And separation is causing this illness
I want to sing and dance with you in the garden
Seeing all creation mirrored in you
Oh moon-face one
I have been seeking your secrets in the night
Hiding away from the night patrol
If they catch me, it will be a hundred lashes
The only pain I want to feel is your nail digging into me
What will you reveal to me?

Bismillahir Rahmanir Raheem

The wise man said
He who looks at the snare is already trapped
So, all it took was one glance of you
And I am already in love.

Bismillahir Rahmanir Raheem

Oh life midday!
Oh festival!
Oh garden of summer!
I wait in restless ecstasy
I stand watch and wait
Where are you, my lover?
It is you I love and wait for
In readiness day and night
Come now!
It is the time you were here!

Bismillahir Rahmanir Raheem

It is to meet you that I am yearning for
Should I give up the ghost and die here in separation?
A hundred thousand prostration given to you
In order to speak
One must first hear
You come to speak by the way of hearing
So, where is your beautiful voice
So that I can hear you like a nightingale is singing to the rose
So that my voice can ascend to the seventh heaven
Where the beloved can hear my lamination
Of union and rejoice of the heart
I have been meditating on the days that we are together
The visual image of you never fades away from my mind
It took one glance from you
But I cannot stop staring
At your body shape and your radiant face
Your brows bent like a bow
Your eyes shoot an arrow straight to my heart
I hold on still like a statue
My heart pumps blood like a water fountain
All this ecstasy, how do I go back to living without you?
It seems an impassable journey
So, I look for a Sufi master
To help me kill the *nafs*
So that when the time comes

I can hold a conversation with you first
That my speaking can go out without difficulties
Even when I know that my will is full of Iblis desires
But love goes beyond good and evil
How can you say what I am doing is wrong
When I am doing it for my beloved?
Every step must be to the one
Dreams make me giddy during the night
I wonder if I love the desire more than what I am desiring.

Bismillahir Rahmanir Raheem

No doubt about that
My heart belongs to thee
It has tasted many a wine
But I can only get intoxicated by yours
You put my head to rest
Without you, I am suffering as Majnun was
Chasing the scent of your tress
From every wind that blows
I am conjuring spells as if I was Solomon
So that I can command the wind
To tell you teals of my love
As distance has kept us apart
You're busy working
And I am busy writing verses for you
In the hope you become a believer
Of this religion of love
And we can jump headlong into the rose garden
Where I can sip your wine
And you can enjoy my morsel
Fulfilled and intertwined
We can overcome this *dunya*
They say the mind has the power
To turn heaven of hell and hell of heaven
I am already suffering through hell
And you're the only one that bring me bliss

My dear congenial,
Nature has given us a long life
If only we know how to use it
So, I choose to spend all my waking hours loving you.

Bismillahir Rahmanir Raheem

In this world of dust
You're the cloud and rain
I am a dried-up meadow
It is you that I need
Long hour in solitude
Lotus flower position
I know that I can climb through the mud
And peak my petals on the water
But ripples of madness have overcome me
I need your soft touch to calm me down
Oh moon-face one
Can you clear a path in this darkness?
Without you, I am just a singing madman
Writing profligate verses.

Bismillahir Rahmanir Raheem

Your touch keeps me free from brain sickness
It sends me frolicking with the dwellers of heaven
How soft and calming it is
How sweat drips like rain in the forest
Growing fruits of delight in my heart
I have sown a hundred thousand verses of sweetness
And your thighs are like trunks of ripe mango trees
Each mouthful makes ecstasy burst out of me
Each stroke is leading me to heaven
My friend, I know you love this agitation
It is better to struggle vainly than to lie still
I want this to last longer
But I cannot hold this joy in any longer
We have been separated for way too long
So my thought of you have grown way too devilish
Should I hold your neck and pin you down?
Oh, sweet voice parrot, caged in my embrace
You will be free once you hit climax
But do not fly too far away
To gain you back, I must throw away grains
In the hope you keep on returning
So I can hear your lullabies
With that voice which is the cry and sound
That indeed is the only voice
And the rest are echoes

I have been hoping for a daily portion
This beggar will keep on asking
In this *dunya* and in Jannah.

Bismillahir Rahmanir Raheem

You, whose beauteous face men were enslaved
How should it be once you are mine?
Would the devil create doubt in my mind?
Causing me to be blind
Not to see your adoration
His monster lurking in the night
Your beauty is that of an idol
And we are all idolaters
I have to watch out as I fight
That I do not turn into a monster
As you gaze long into the abyss
The abyss also gazes into you
So, I must push through the dirt
So I can be pure for you
Oh, my dear beloved,
Don't you know
That under conditions of peace
The war like man attack himself
I do not want to lose you
In my own ignorance
So, I meditate throughout the day
So I can embrace you in the night
You are my only desire.

Bismillahir Rahmanir Raheem

I have become non-existent in thy existence
Because I am thy lover
Love makes blind and deaf
I cannot hear the saints' guidance
As I follow this path of an idolater
You're the light
And my body is a prism
My madness is the many light that come out
There are so many ways into bewilderment
When I am loving you
Which skirt should I grab?
So that I am led a straight
Your jealously is vast
So what is a dervish master
When I can lay with you
You cause the world to crumble
If I think of any other but you, my beloved.

Bismillahir Rahmanir Raheem

It is said
That whatsoever a man soweth, that shall he also reap
So I am writing verses and displaying acts of generosity
In the hope that my lamentation reaches you
And you can see this poor beggar at your door steps
I give thanks to the beloved for my daily bread
So that I can keep my focus in praying for you
One day this distance will be reduced
And we can be joined together
Will that be the day before the trumpets?
Only time can tell
What is written is already written
But patience I have
As I have been thinking of you
From the day I caught your glance
How wonderful will it be
If I can have you in this world and the world to come.

Bismillahir Rahmanir Raheem

I produce fresh milk from the sugar
I mingle milk and honey with my verses
But it seems I can't pull you any closer
And the distance still feels oh so far apart
What more is it to do?
But kill the *nafs*
And only have you in my existence
Meditation after meditation
The journey is life long
And I do not have a guide
But your face in my remembrance
That is enough for me to carry on
But I wish I pull down the veil
And see the secrets of the night
That will keep Iblis at bay
As every beauty is thy beauty
And the gaze has been wondering
Hoping to fulfil what you have left
And with time the ambers have burnt bright
Am I truly made of straw?
Or would I be able to handle this ache
Of dear beloved, give me patience
So that I can be with the one
Who keeps me up late at night writing verses of love

Bismillahir Rahmanir Raheem

Oh, dear Mrs Shiva
I am thy charmer
I have been casting spells
And like a snake
You have been casting them back
Will you enter this snare
Or will I take a bite?
There is poison in the almond cake
So I aim to be a saint
The saint is he who is the antidote
So go on biting
And I will calmly mirror your dancing
Until these spells take you away from him
And I call you mine.

Bismillahir Rahmanir Raheem

How love: saucy, uncontrolled and restless
Throw my whole body into madness
How I wish for just a morsel of you
So I can lose conscious
If I get more than my fill
I shall pass away into Jannah
The wind blows
And the only fragrance is you
I am Solomon
I watch the nightingale sing to the rose
All those love songs
Causes the heart to flatter
I am Majnun
I see your face in all sixteen directions
Prostrations till the knees bleed
It is the only way to worship you.

Bismillahir Rahmanir Raheem

Without head or foot, I would be journeying
Like a hermit in the mountain
I have excluded myself from the unbelievers
Where your body is, that is my *qibla*
Faced with obstacles, your face clears them
Blind, deaf and dumb, I will be following you
Give me the order, no matter the distance
They say love gives motion to the spirit
And I have lost my body in loving you
What is this existence without being loved by you?
The day you accept these verses
Without lip or tooth, I would be eating sugar
Knowing that you're mine
I start planting these roses in the garden
So we can frolic like Adam and Eve
Without shame or veils between us
I curse the devil whilst drinking this apple juice
Knowing without spiritual knowledge
How could I have obtained you.

Bismillahir Rahmanir Raheem

If I gain access to you
I will become a king
How long shall misfortune befall me
As long as I am away from you
I am still 'I'
A madman who writes verses
A madman who is deeply in love
The double end of thread is not for the needle
So how should I enter your door with an I?
Absence and separation has kept me raw
Touch me with your flames, so I can become cooked
And enter into your kingdom
The place where I drop my I
By your hand every impossible thing is made possible
By fear of losing you my madness is made quite
Every lover is saying this
But who, what will deliver him from hypocrisy?

Bismillahir Rahmanir Raheem

In your presence neither madness
Nor soundness of understanding remains
Bewildered by your beauty
You stop the cunning fox
So, I curse the devil and hold his hand
I need him to act
Wicked thoughts, reduced to a beast
But I am more than human
When it comes to pleasing you
This is the realm between existence and non-existence
We are at the beginning
Let it be a big bang
First, I see the face
Then you drop the veil
Oh what a secret you've been hiding
I can't comprehend it
But I can practice it
Like a hypocrite, I think myself deserving.

Bismillahir Rahmanir Raheem

Oh moon-face one
You say all this is blasphemy
But let me tell you
That it is better to sin first
And sacrifice afterward
As no one but you know my intention
And the accursed one has took away my patience
So, if I pluck the rose and kiss it after
With enough lamentation
God will forgive me
Let us be repenting sinners
We learn through making errors
I don't want to call it an error as it is so sweet
But before being united with you
It is frowned upon
The ones who call themselves noble
Are nothing but hypocrites on the way
Full of devilish thoughts
Just like me and you
But I am a Solomon
Who has commanded his jinn
I said bring that throne
You're my queen of Sheba
Now accept the religion of love
Get intoxicated with me
And move your body in the darkest night.

Bismillahir Rahmanir Raheem

Like an ant
I am so happy in this granary
That I am dragging a burden too great for me
Pursuing you is not an easy task
But it brings me pleasure to write these verses
Knowing that one day, I will be united with you
So I go back and forth into my subconsciousness
To find the words to utter in lamentation
Oh I am dragging more than my body weight
Of the goodness in my mind
So I can shower you with pearls
Oh my mind is the ocean
And my verses are the foam
One creates the other
I hope they land on your shore
So you can take pleasure in an unveiling
This is only my truth
You're a goddess
And I want access to your thighs
Before you question me
Know that I am a lover of the whole
Not just the part
As the lover of the part
Can never obtain the whole.

Bismillahir Rahmanir Raheem

I asked what is love
You said that I will know once I am lost in thee
I am holding thy skirt
Travelling into non-existence
I am fixated by thy mole
Describing the whole of you will take eternity
I now know that this is love
As your image does not leave my mind
I give up wage earning
So I can have time to write these verses
They are a description of my longing for thee
I am not I but you
My body does not move
Unless it is by doing thy deed.

Bismillahir Rahmanir Raheem

You have bound my eye
With the spell of tress and mole
Wherever I look, you're all that I see
You're the beauty in the rose
You're the beauty in the moon
You're all the beautiful things
Your tress flows like the River Nile
Your skin glows like cocoa beans
Your mole perfectly placed just above the lip
Your brows bent pleasingly
Your eyes are as pretty as andalusite
I am gazing into an abyss
And that abyss is gazing back
There is no way of escaping your snare
Would rather die in love with you.

Bismillahir Rahmanir Raheem

By your love, bitter things become sweet
By your love, pieces of copper become gold
By your love, dregs become clear
By your love, pain becomes healing
Your love is the only thing needed
To live in ecstasy and bliss.

Bismillahir Rahmanir Raheem

Oh God!
Either let me not come to speech at all
Or give me leave to tell the whole to the end
I have only shown my suffering through separation
And only describe my love for you
May you allow the deaf to hear my lamentation
So that a bridge can be created between two hearts
And that we can travel on the right path
I want to end up in the rose garden
Where the sun shines
So I can sip your wine
And dance fiercely with the beloved
Till the moon illuminates the dark night
Where union with you is promised by saints such as Rumi
Who I followed his word till I learn to create my own
Astaghfirullah, astaghfirullah, astaghfirullah
Astaghfirullah a hundred thousand times
The pen has been weak but with time it will get stronger.